NURTURING
The
American Dream

◆

Frank PN Adjei-Mensah

authorHOUSE

AuthorHouse™
1663 Liberty Drive
Bloomington, IN 47403
www.authorhouse.com
Phone: 833-262-8899

Illustrated and Cover designed by Daniel O Adjei-Mensah
DAMKOS Design, England UK.

Published by AuthorHouse 07/09/2024

ISBN: 978-1-5246-5684-3 (sc)
ISBN: 978-1-5246-5686-7 (hc)
ISBN: 978-1-5246-5685-0 (e)

Library of Congress Control Number: 2016921127

Print information available upon request.

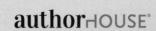

A message from our Sponsor

It is our firm belief and noble commitment to educate our children in a manner that equip them well in harnessing their creative potential, as well as the financial wherewithal that will nurture their imaginations into upstanding adulthood.

We believe this is arguably the single most important investment that anybody or government, anywhere in the world , could make for the next generation towards its development and prosperity. We are in this spirit proudly sponsoring this wholesome book so that no child is left uninformed about the sure path to their future success.

THE YOU

NURTURE THE DREAM

ASSETS

Aim High

Turn Ideas into Income

INFORMATION AGE

Innovate

Think BIG

Dream even BIGGER

Frank P.N. ADJEI-MENSAH, BA (Hons, Law & Sociology). He is an upstanding and active member of his community and a remarkable motivational speaker. He is also the author of The American Dream Declassified.

FINANCIAL FREEDOM

ASSETS ACQUISITION

Creativity

THE BLUEPRINT

Imaginative

Be Industrious

Persist with diligence.

FOLLOW YOUR DREAMS

Be Bold

NURTURE THE DREAM

Aim High

ASSETS

Turn Ideas into Income

INFORMATION AGE

Think BIG

Dream even

BIGGER

FINANCIAL FREEDOM

ASSETS
ACQUISITION

Creativity

THE
BLUEPRINT

Imaginative

Be Industrious

Persist with diligence

FOLLOW YOUR DREAMS

Be Bold

NURTURE THE DREAM

ASSETS

Aim High

Turn Ideas into Income

INFORMATION AGE

Innovate

B
L
U
E
P
R
I
N
T

T
H
E

Think BIG

B
L
U
E
P
R
I
N
T

T
H
E

Dream even
BIGGER

ASSETS
ACQUISITION

FINANCIAL FREEDOM

Creativity

THE
BLUEPRINT

Imaginative

Be Industrious

Persist with diligence

FOLLOW YOUR DREAMS

Be Bold

Meet Nigel. A fine, young, up-and-coming "American-Dreamer."

1

When Nigel was little he enjoyed playing with his toys quite a lot.

On several occasions when any of his toys broke down, he'd hunker down to fix it himself.

Occasionally, he'd seek his dad's advice on how to fix his toys.

Now, meet Cody. Nigel's best friend.

Nigel and Cody have been playmates and buddies since childhood.

They attended the same elementary school.

They were in the same class from first grade.

They both did great in school and enjoyed their school work as much as their playtime.

Like Cody, Nigel didn't play with his homework. He was a serious student.

Most days, he'd ask his parents for help with his homework.

Some days, Nigel and Cody would meet-up to do their homework together as study-mates.

They liked playing outside too, doing bike racing and stunts.

At times they'd skate-board for a while.............

...........or ride their hoverboards around the neighborhood, and just goof-off till they return home tired. Talk about an active lifestyle.

They liked to watch TV and play video games sometimes.

Nigel's toys always got his attention. He was greatly impressed with how cleverly they'd been put together.

He grew so curious with his toys. Occasionally he'd take them apart, then put them back together.

Nigel started making his own toy cars, trains, and planes with Styrofoam, cardboard, glue, and other materials.

He'd color them artfully with oil paint.

He liked to spend some time on his art projects #daily, no matter how tired he felt, before going to bed. He was #focused and #determined to finish stuff he started.

This became a habit over the years. A good and vitally important habit which would help him achieve his dreams sooner or later.

Nigel liked to show-off his new models to Cody who admired them a lot.

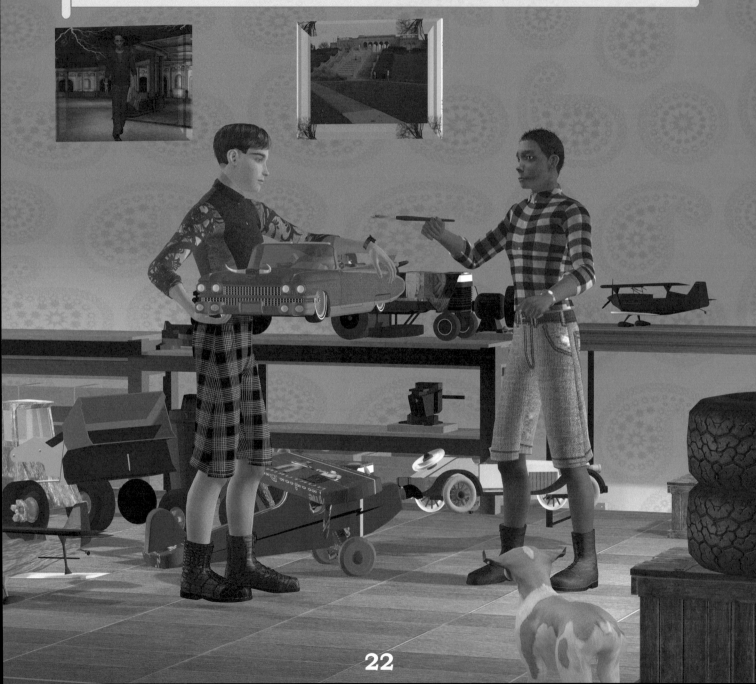

Cody encouraged Nigel. He'd sometimes bring his own toys to re-decorate them with help from his friend Nigel, the artist.

Nigel liked to put up his latest pieces on display to his classmates during "show-and-tell." They also admired them greatly.

They were always excited to see his latest, slick designs.

They'd bug him to make some crazy, eye-catching models for them as well.

Nigel was kept busy as more and more friends showed interest in his work. Some were even inspired to do something creative themselves.

Nigel's parents worried that the hobby might affect his school studies and grades, but it really didn't at all.

With help from his parents, Nigel was able to balance his school work with his hobby and playtime.

He was still making straight A's just like his buddy, Cody.

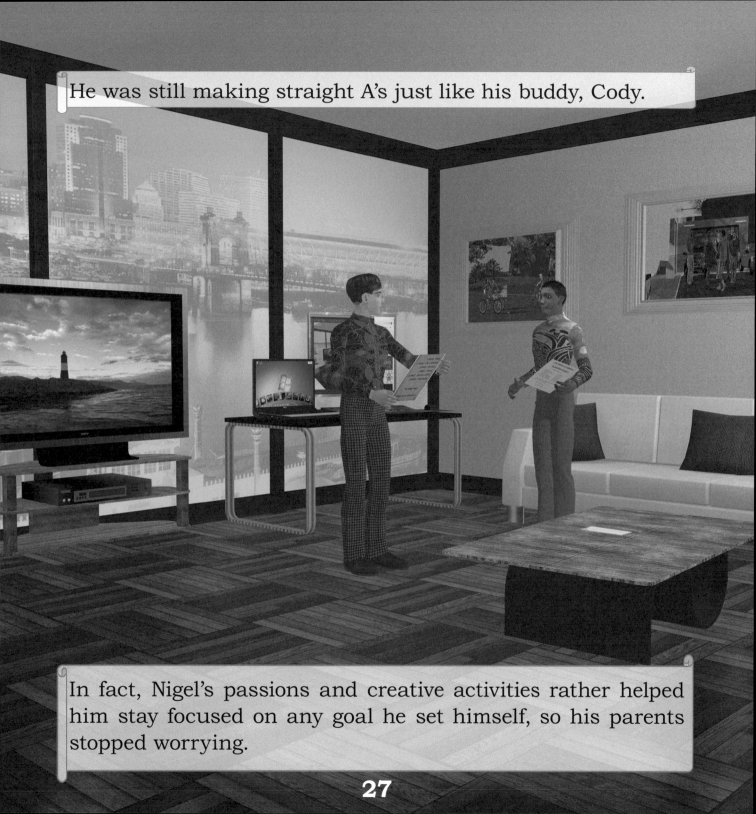

In fact, Nigel's passions and creative activities rather helped him stay focused on any goal he set himself, so his parents stopped worrying.

They were, however, curious to see where this hobby might lead.

They were eager to give Nigel all the encouragement, help, and supervision he needed to enjoy his passion and fulfill his dreams.

Nigel kept working on his toy projects, day in and day out.

He kept perfecting his creative skills on his toys, even providing custom styles and finishes for his friends.

Nigel attracted many fans to his fantastic, cool pieces.

Cheers for his creativity came from everywhere, including friends, schoolmates, adults and parents.

Some parents from the neighborhood often ordered "Nigel Brand" toys for their kids.

With time, Nigel started mailing out sets of parts for assembling his brand toys.

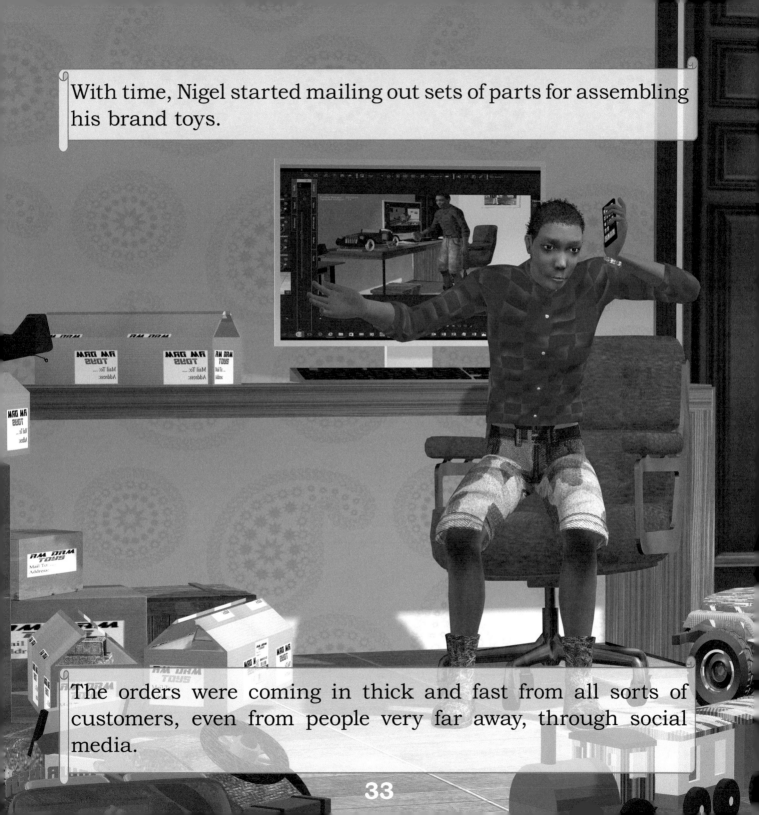

The orders were coming in thick and fast from all sorts of customers, even from people very far away, through social media.

Nigel began to seriously consider making a great business out of his crafts.

Nigel often sought Cody's advice and views on his toy business.

The two friends often shared ideas on their passions and hobbies.

Cody's passions were in biology and chemistry. He was very curious and fascinated by stuff in those subjects.

He dreamt of becoming a pharmacist.

Nigel often sought his parents' advice also on his business ideas and career.

His parents always advised him to put his school work first, for now. They, however, gave him all the advice and encouragement to pursue his creative talents.

They felt proud and amazed at his creativity, and had a hunch that something might actually come out of it.

Nigel always received good and critical feedback on his craftsmanship from his great friend, Cody......

39

...from his parents....

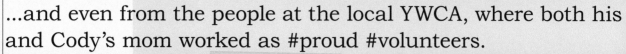

...and even from the people at the local YWCA, where both his and Cody's mom worked as #proud #volunteers.

Nigel started researching on the Internet about the process of toy-making, and the companies that make them.

He even sent out some of his latest designs to a few companies that he found, to see if they could make them in large numbers.

Nigel was overjoyed and couldn't contain his happiness.

He'd just received the terrific news he'd been waiting for, a positive response from a toy manufacturer.

Nigel hurried downstairs, with his mom hot on his heels, to break the good news to his parents.

Nigel then took a deep breath and told himself to just relax. A toy manufacturer had agreed to reproduce his designs in large numbers, after several gut-wrenching turndowns.

He went on to explain that the company gave him two options.

They offered to either make the toys, sell them and pay him monthly, called #royalties, or send him the toys and allow him to find stores that would buy them.

Nigel couldn't wait to break this wonderful news to his friend, Cody. Dream (Nigel's dog) got a li'l excited with some puppies as they strolled the neighborhood.

With advice from his parents, Nigel decided to collect the monthly royalties from the company rather, so he could stay focused on his school work.

Nigel received his first royalty check at the beginning of summer when he turned fifteen.

He was thrilled, and proudly showed the check to his parents.

The entire Philips household was filled with joy.

Nigel and Cody headed off to college as freshmen when they turned 18.

Nigel went to college to become a school teacher.

Cody earned admission to study pharmacy, following his passion for chemistry and biology.

Nigel's parents didn't have to worry about college tuition fees. The royalty checks took care of all his fees and expenses.

This was a welcome relief for a family with its own financial struggles.

Nigel continued to increase his assets by designing more of his fancy toys in his spare times, even while in college.

Nigel and Cody hung out regularly at home during school breaks.

They'd fill each other in on their experiences on college campuses.

Nigel and Cody often went out to town for a meal with their friends.

Nigel was already earning so much from his royalty payments, and he was even investing part of his earnings in stocks of some stable and profitable companies to earn more money.

They'd chit-chat about their progress in college.

Cody once wanted to know how Nigel's toy business was coming along.

Nigel was more than happy to tell them about his latest, terrific designs. He told his friends how the royalty payments were building up his savings and increasing his wealth.

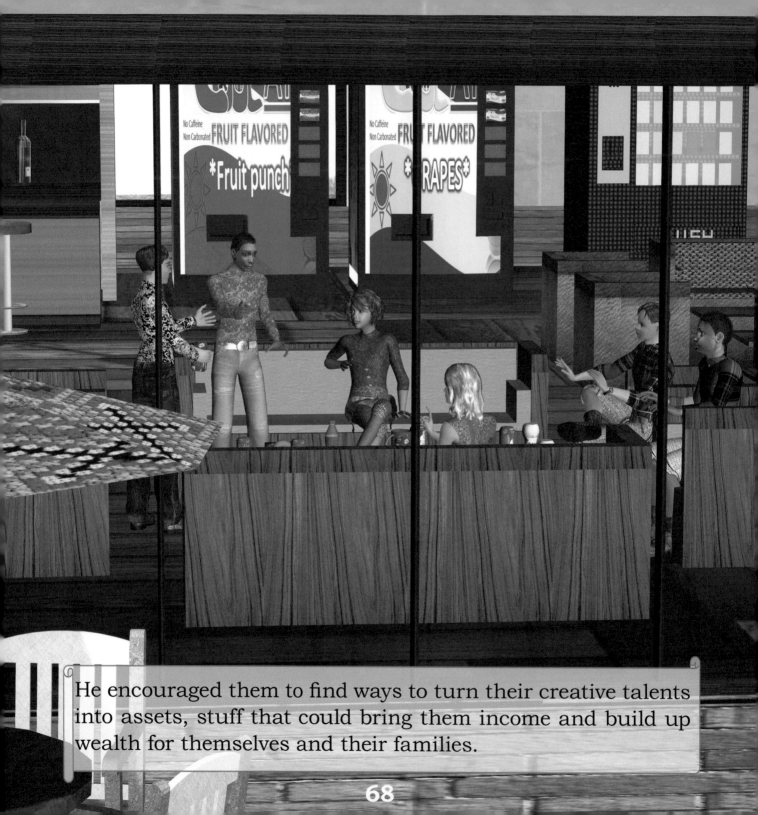

He encouraged them to find ways to turn their creative talents into assets, stuff that could bring them income and build up wealth for themselves and their families.

Nigel and Cody are all grown-up now.

69

Nigel married his college sweetheart, Maya. They have three kids.

The eldest is ten year old LeBron, then eight year old Nigel Jr., and little Rachel who is six.

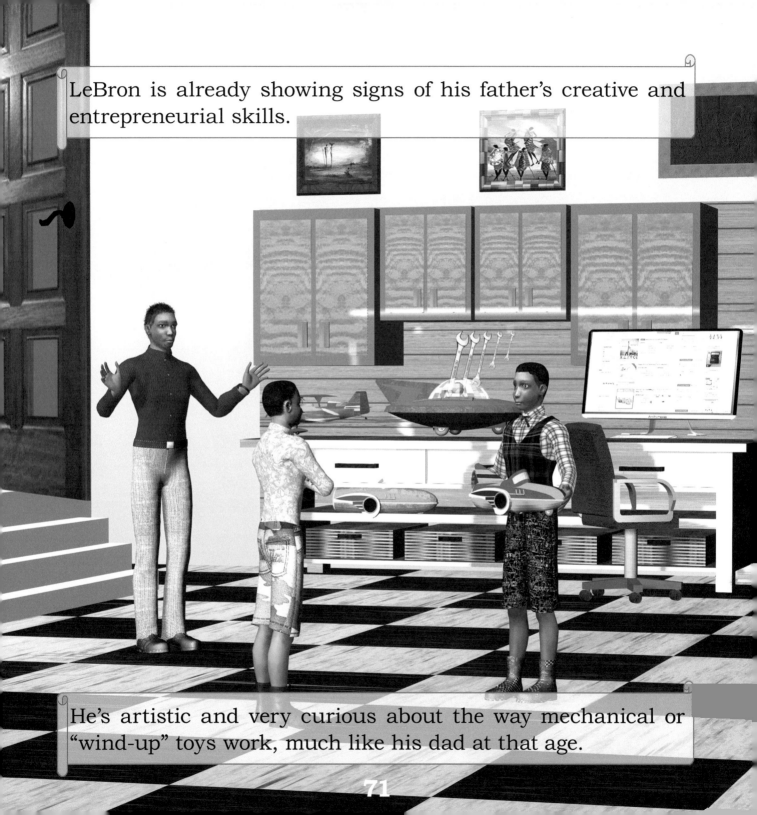

LeBron is already showing signs of his father's creative and entrepreneurial skills.

He's artistic and very curious about the way mechanical or "wind-up" toys work, much like his dad at that age.

Nigel Jr., on the other hand, is a very creative storyteller already. He likes imaginative writing, and his teachers are very impressed with him.

Little Rachel, for now, is all about play-acting with her toys and being dotted-on by her parents.

She plays video games on her tablet sometimes, and talks about creating her own games very soon. She was introduced to coding at a very early age. She's so eager to build something great, with "Silicon Valley" on her young mind already.

Cody has graduated and is now a pharmacist. He's doing very well at his job, and is well paid.

Cody is very happy with his profession, and well content with his personal life.

Cody got married to Hilary, his sweetheart he met at a job as an intern. They have two children now; Josh and Mavis.

Josh is ten years and looks just like his dad. He's already a "semi-pro" coder. He can create some amazing stuff on the computer, like an absolute boss!

Mavis is eight, and quite simply a delight to hang around. She wants to be a pediatrician like her aunt, Dr. Helen, who also #owns a bunch of restaurants.

Cody and his family live in a nice house ....

.....with beautiful lawns, a swimming pool and a large backyard for children to play.

Cody's family enjoys all the modern home comforts......

....with furnishings, gadgets and toys for the kids to play with, including some latest "Nigel Brand" toys.

Nigel and his family, the Philips, also purchased a nice house in the same quiet, cozy suburb as Cody.

They enjoy modern home comforts and luxury stuff as well.

The two families often get together to socialize, discuss their plans, and just have fun.

They also discuss problems and issues that bother them, and seek each other's advice.

The two moms, Maya and Hilary, are both studying for their Masters degrees. They usually spend times like this #brainstorming for #ideas to work on together after graduation.

Nigel and Cody's families once vacationed on a tropical beach.

84

As time went by, Cody seemed to complain way too often about money, even though his salary was much higher than Nigel's.

He'd complain about how he could no longer afford the summer vacation trips they used to take to Mexico, Jamaica, Africa and other places.

He craved all the fun they had at the Kumasi Zoo, for example.

He also complained a lot about bills, and wasn't sure if he could ever retire from work and live comfortably.

His retirement savings weren't coming along all that great, he said.

Cody's complaints would just go on and on, all about financial problems.

Nigel's usual response was to remind him to never depend totally on his salary. Create #ASSETS that could fetch extra income for you and your family, and even grandkids and so on, he'd say.

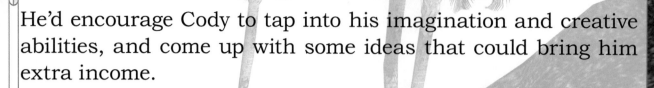

He'd encourage Cody to tap into his imagination and creative abilities, and come up with some ideas that could bring him extra income.

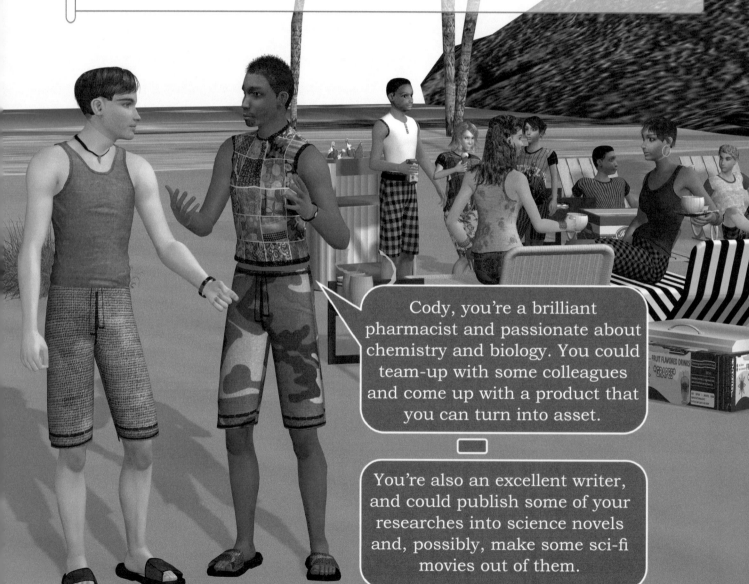

Cody, you're a brilliant pharmacist and passionate about chemistry and biology. You could team-up with some colleagues and come up with a product that you can turn into asset.

You're also an excellent writer, and could publish some of your researches into science novels and, possibly, make some sci-fi movies out of them.

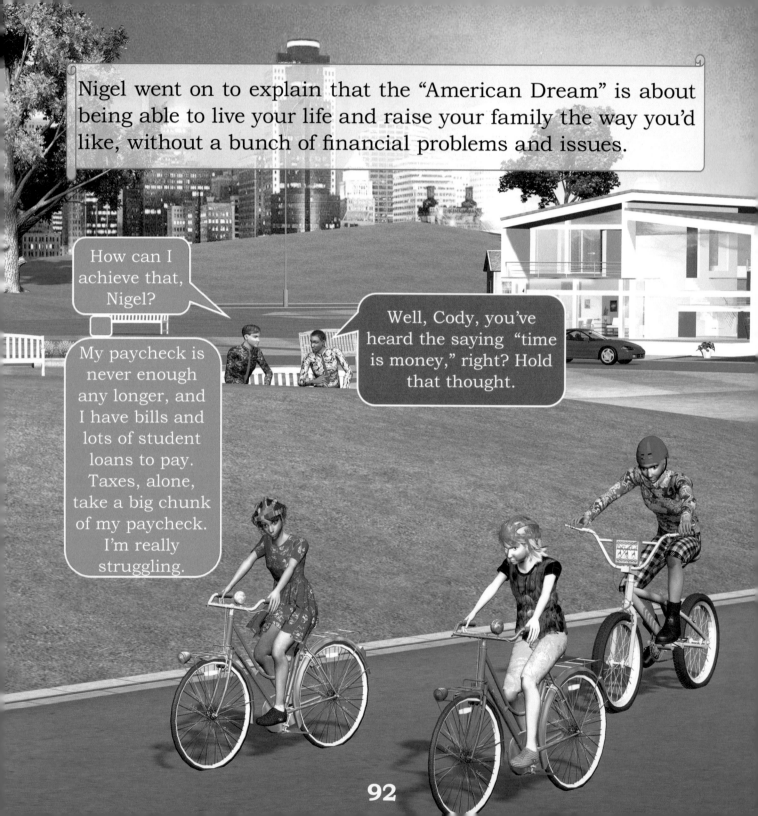

Nigel went on to explain that the "American Dream" is about being able to live your life and raise your family the way you'd like, without a bunch of financial problems and issues.

How can I achieve that, Nigel?

My paycheck is never enough any longer, and I have bills and lots of student loans to pay. Taxes, alone, take a big chunk of my paycheck. I'm really struggling.

Well, Cody, you've heard the saying "time is money," right? Hold that thought.

Here's one reason, Cody. Most people work and earn a living 8-hours per day on the job. That means they earn no income in the remaining sixteen hours that they're not working, Nigel explained.

Are you asking me to work around the clock, non-stop, Nigel? Cody asked anxiously.

Far from that actually, Nigel replied. That's impossible!

As I've been telling you, it simply means you must apply your creativity and imagination to create #value in a product or service that people, governments, or organisations would like to buy or pay for, even people from around the world. This could fetch you income around the clock, whether you're asleep, sick /disabled, on vacation, or even lose your job for whatever reason, he explained further.

You begin by coming up with an #IDEA, and start working on it. Then, sooner or later, you could bring other people, workers and experts on board to work on the idea or project.

That way, your time could soon be freed-up to spend with your family and friends, raising your children, traveling and having fun. Your finances could also be much more secured as well, Nigel continued.

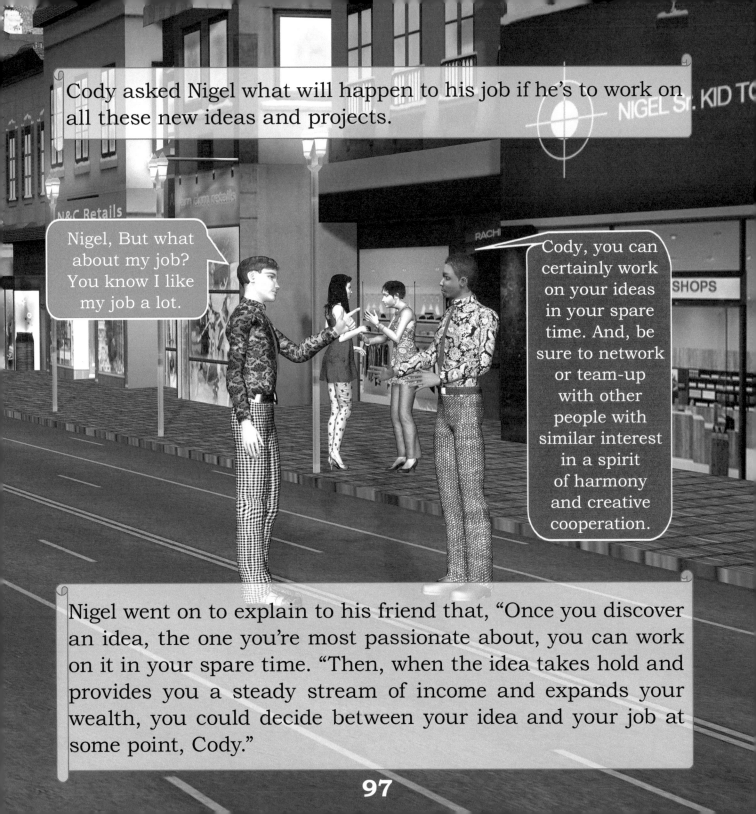

Cody asked Nigel what will happen to his job if he's to work on all these new ideas and projects.

Nigel, But what about my job? You know I like my job a lot.

Cody, you can certainly work on your ideas in your spare time. And, be sure to network or team-up with other people with similar interest in a spirit of harmony and creative cooperation.

Nigel went on to explain to his friend that, "Once you discover an idea, the one you're most passionate about, you can work on it in your spare time. "Then, when the idea takes hold and provides you a steady stream of income and expands your wealth, you could decide between your idea and your job at some point, Cody."

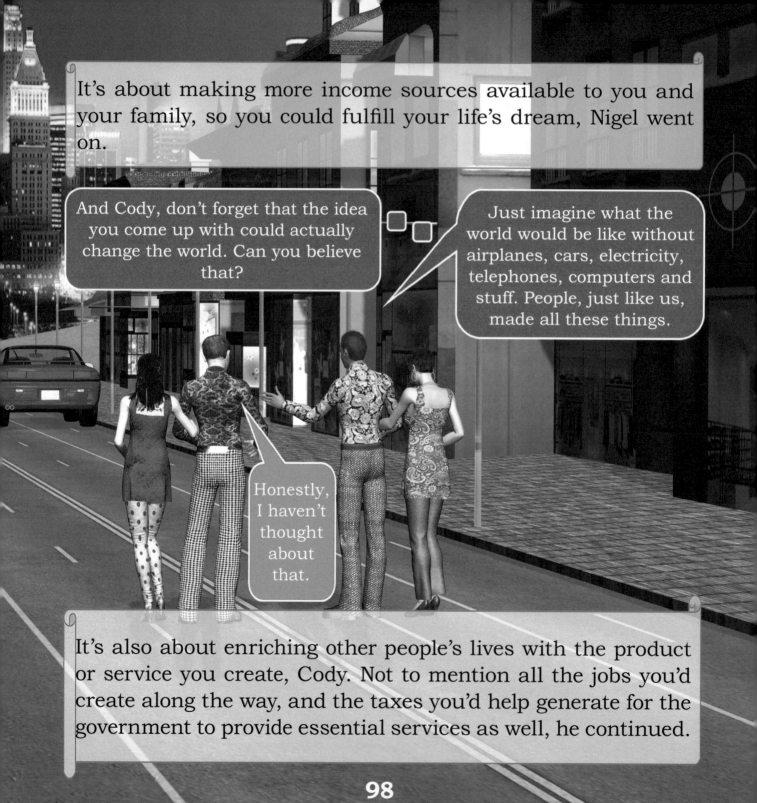

It's about making more income sources available to you and your family, so you could fulfill your life's dream, Nigel went on.

And Cody, don't forget that the idea you come up with could actually change the world. Can you believe that?

Just imagine what the world would be like without airplanes, cars, electricity, telephones, computers and stuff. People, just like us, made all these things.

Honestly, I haven't thought about that.

It's also about enriching other people's lives with the product or service you create, Cody. Not to mention all the jobs you'd create along the way, and the taxes you'd help generate for the government to provide essential services as well, he continued.

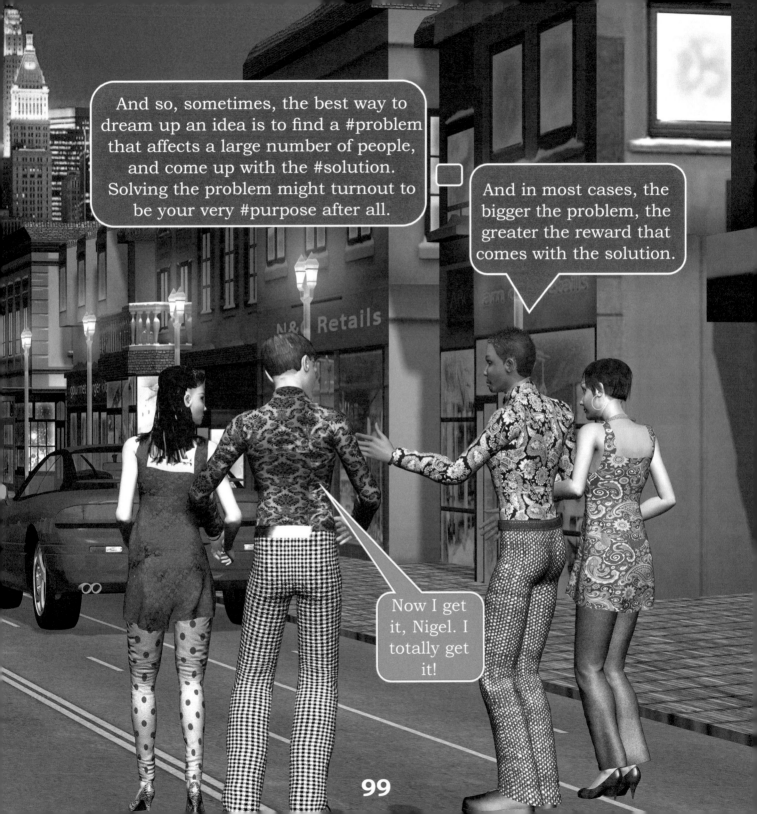

By the way, Allison and Nia went on to the same college, graduated, then set up the A&N Apps & Coding Academy, Nigel continued.

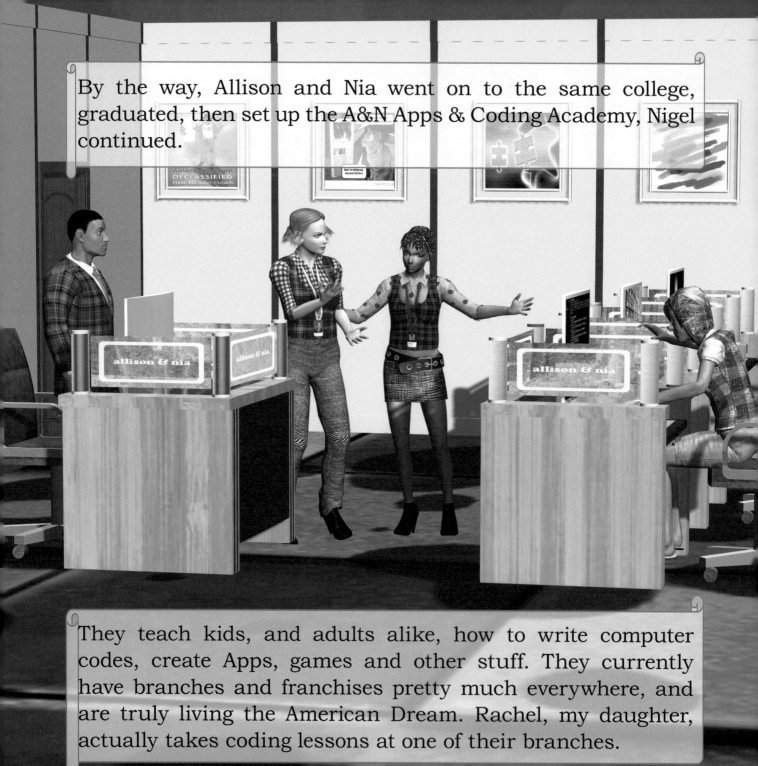

They teach kids, and adults alike, how to write computer codes, create Apps, games and other stuff. They currently have branches and franchises pretty much everywhere, and are truly living the American Dream. Rachel, my daughter, actually takes coding lessons at one of their branches.

Nigel, meanwhile, continues to design toys in his spare times, which the toy manufacturer promptly makes them and sends to markets around the world.

Nigel and his family have no worries about money at all, and he can retire from his cherished teaching job whenever he decides. He has achieved Financial Freedom.

He tells Cody, that some of his proudest moments is when he travels, like say, to other countries, and sees children having fun with toys he designed.

All his children have taken after him. They use their spare times to work on little projects from their own imaginations.

The times they spend on their projects and ideas are actually fun, exciting, and yes, #challenging. Everybody looks forward to and enjoys it anyway.

Nigel has actually instilled in them that "#Personal Initiative," that is, taking important steps and actions without waiting to be told, is the #cornerstone of personal #success and wealth creation. And that, it's better to develop this essential habit earlier in their lives.

Listen, kiddos. You, like every kid, have the potential and ability to change the world, and make it a better place by the ideas you come up with to solve problems and create value for people.

You may also question why things are the way they are, and ask yourself HOW #you could make them better. Indeed, you may question, just about, everything. It's called Innovation, and could make you very wealthy.

He inspires them.

He cautions them, however, against bad and unnecessary #spending habits and #debts when they grow up. He says, those could hold them back from achieving their dreams.

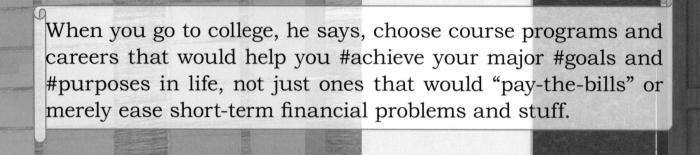

When you go to college, he says, choose course programs and careers that would help you #achieve your major #goals and #purposes in life, not just ones that would "pay-the-bills" or merely ease short-term financial problems and stuff.

He advises them.

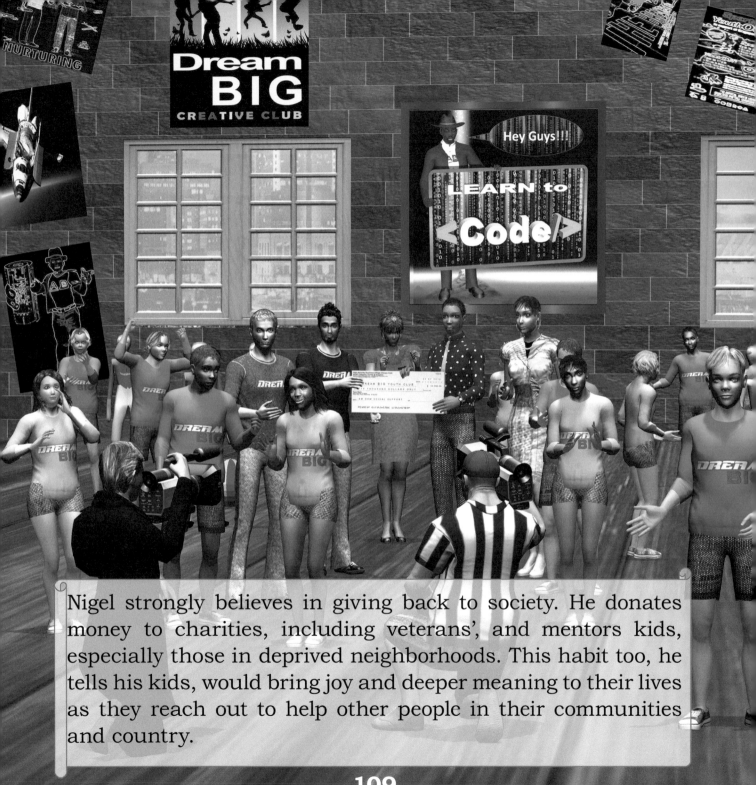

Nigel strongly believes in giving back to society. He donates money to charities, including veterans', and mentors kids, especially those in deprived neighborhoods. This habit too, he tells his kids, would bring joy and deeper meaning to their lives as they reach out to help other people in their communities and country.

One evening, Nigel was mentoring a group of kids. He advised them that, pursuing great dreams and goals could be difficult and challenging. That, #persistence, #passion, #hardworking, great #commitment, #positive-mental-attitude, and strong #belief in one's ability to meet challenges and succeed, are crucial for worthy achievements above mediocrity. You must.........

Just then his phone rung, and he answered. It was Cody on the line. He was calling to invite Nigel and his family to an international award winning ceremony for scientific breakthrough in honor of himself and his partners.

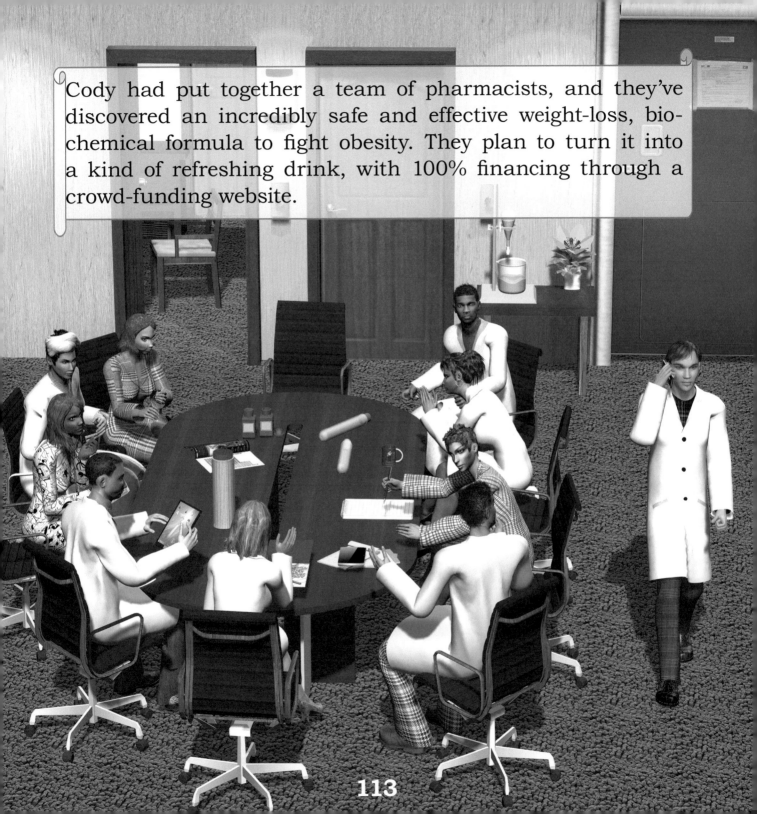

Cody had put together a team of pharmacists, and they've discovered an incredibly safe and effective weight-loss, bio-chemical formula to fight obesity. They plan to turn it into a kind of refreshing drink, with 100% financing through a crowd-funding website.

Nigel accepted the invitation with cheers, and he's so pumped up to witness this historic event to honor his friend. He believes this would further inspire his own kids to dream BIGGER as well.

Two months later, here they are on the BIG stage. Cody and his partners receiving their award, amidst cheers and congratulations.

Nigel was right. His kids are super-duper excited and inspired by the event they've just witnessed.

He assures them that creating value and solving problems are, arguably, the most certain pathways to truly achieve the #AMERICANDREAM.

DIFFICULTIES MASTERED...

..ARE OPPORTUNITIES WON.

"Winston Churchill"

NURTURING The American Dream

ASSETS

The Workbook

Aim High

Turn Ideas into Income

INFORMATION AGE

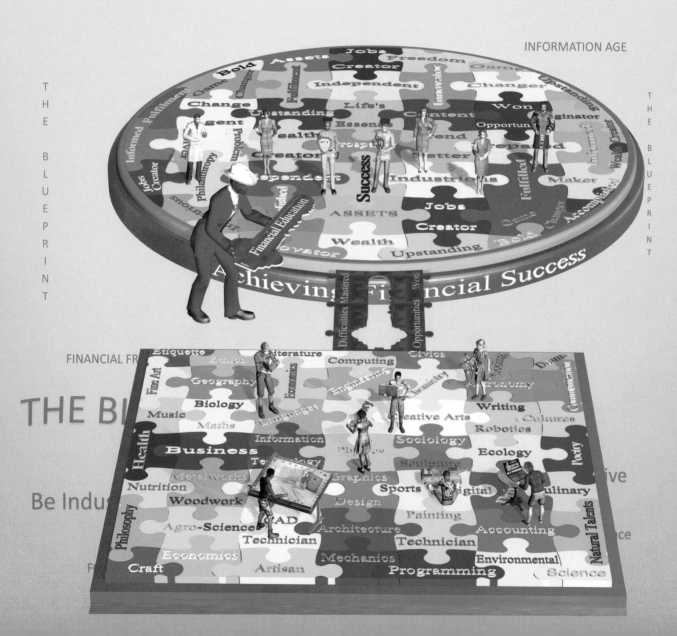

CAPTURE THE DREAM

Think High

Think BIG

FINANCIAL FREEDOM

THE BLUEPR

Be Industrious

FOLLOW YOUR DREAMS

1. What Is Your Dream, And How Do You Plan On Fulfilling It?

2. Is Your Dream BIG Enough That It Scares You Sometimes?

2

3. What Is An Asset? Give Examples.

4. Does An Asset Bring You Income Or Take Money From You?

5. What Is A Liability? Give Examples.

6. Does A Liability Bring You Income Or Take Money From You?

DREAM

Innovate

Think BIG

FINANCIAL FREEDOM

THE BLUEPRINT

Be Industrious

FOLLOW YOUR DREAMS

7. Why Should You Strive To Increase Your Assets And Keep Your Liabilities As Low As Possible?

Turn Ideas into Income

INFORMATION AGE

Dream even BIGGER

ASSETS ACQUISITION

Creativity

Imaginative

Persist with diligence

Be Bold

NURTURE THE DREAM

High

Innovate

Think BIG

FINANCIAL FREEDOM

THE BLUEPRINT

Be Industrious

FOLLOW YOUR DREAMS

8. What is "Purpose"?

ASSETS

Turn Ideas into Income

INFORMATION AGE

Dream even BIGGER

ASSETS ACQUISITION

Creativity

Imaginative

Persist with diligence

Be Bold

THE DREAM

Innovate

Think BIG

FINANCIAL FREEDOM

THE BLUEPRINT

Be Industrious

9. What Is Your Purpose, And How Do You Plan On Fulfilling It?

Turn Ideas into Income

INFORMATION AGE

Dream even BIGGER

ASSETS ACQUISITION

Creativity

Imaginative

Persist with diligence

Be Bold

ASSETS

Turn Ideas into Income

INFORMATION AGE

Innovate

Dream even BIGGER

ASSETS ACQUISITION

Creativity

Imaginative

Persist with diligence

Be Bold

THE DREAM

gh

Think BIG

FINANCIAL FREEDOM

THE BLUEPRINT

Be Industrious

FOLLOW YOUR DREAMS

11. Do You See Problems As Opportunities For Progress Or Issues To Avoid?

12. Is There A Problem In Your Community, Country, Or The World That Bothers You A Lot?

14. Have You Considered Solving That Problem Yourself?

Yes:		No:	
Other			

15. If You Answered Yes, Do You Need Specialized Knowledge To Be Able To Solve The Problem?

16. Where Do You Think You Could Acquire Such Knowledge?

Innovate

Think BIG

Turn Ideas into Income

INFORMATION AGE

Dream even BIGGER

ASSETS ACQUISITION

FINANCIAL FREEDOM

Creativity

THE BLUEPRINT

Imaginative

Be Industrious

Persist with diligence

FOLLOW YOUR DREAMS

Be Bold

17. Would You Consider Going To College To Acquire That Specialized Knowledge?

18.   What Actions Are You Currently Taking Towards Solving That Problem?

19. Do You Have A Talent Or Gift You Can Use To Help Solve The Problem?

20. Do You Have, Or Have You Thought About Forming A Team Of Various Talents To Help Solve The Problem?

21. Do You Think Finance For The Project Would Be An Issue?

22. Have You Considered "Crowd-Funding."

23. Do You Understand The Importance Of Maintaining Good Credit For Your Overall Financial Health?

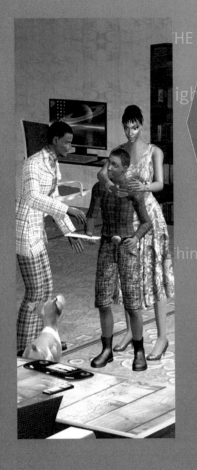

24. Would Your Solution To The Problem Make Your Community, Country, And The World A Better Place To Live?

25. How Would Your Solution To The Problem Benefit You And Your Family?

26. Would Your Solution To The Problem Result In Creating Jobs For Others?

27. Would You Commit To Solving The Problem (Providing Value) Better Than Anyone Could In Terms Of Quality?

28. Would You Commit To Solving The Problem However Long It Would Take?

29. What Would You Do To Avoid The Problem Of Procrastination, Wasting Time?

30. Which Habits Would You Cultivate To Ensure Your Success?

31. Do You Have, Or Would You Seek Help From A Mentor?

32. Would You Commit To Abiding By The Law In Every Step Of Your Project?

NURTURE THE DREAM

Aim High

Think BIG

FINANCIAL FREEDOM

THE BLUEPRINT

Be Industrious

FOLLOW YOUR DREAM

33. Would You Commit To Charitable Donations As A Way Of Paying It Forward?

34. "Education Is THE KEY To Success." What Do You Understand By That?

NURTURE THE DREAM

Aim High

Innovate

Think BIG

Dream even BIGGER

THE BLUEPRINT

ASSET ACQUISITION

FINANCIAL FREEDOM

Creativity

THE BLUEPRINT

Be Industrious

FOLLOW YOUR DREAM

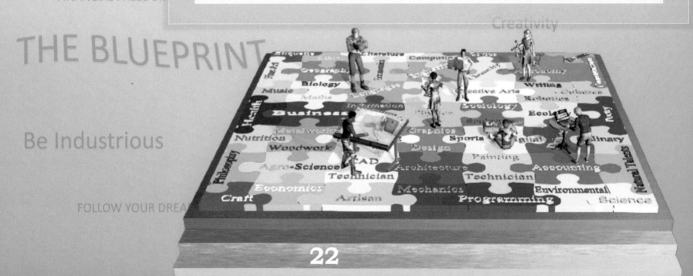

NURTURE THE DREAM

Aim High

H
E
B
L
N
T

Think BIG

FINANCIAL FREEDOM

THE BLUEPRINT

Be Industrious

 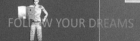

FOLLOW YOUR DREAMS

35. "Financial Education Is THE KEY To Financial Success." What Do You Understand By That?

Turn Ideas into Income

INFORMATION AGE

Innovate

Dream even BIGGER

Assets ACQUISITION

Creativity

Imaginative

Persist with diligence

Be Bold

23

NURTURE THE DREAM

Aim High

Think BIG

FINANCIAL FREEDOM

THE BLUEPRINT

Be Industrious

FOLLOW YOUR DREAMS

Innovate

Dream even BIGGER

Turn Ideas into Income

INFORMATION AGE

Creativity

Imaginative

Persist with diligence

Be Bold

36. Do You See Failures As Part Of The Learning Process, Or Simply A Reason To Quit?

37. Do You See Risk-taking As Necessary For Success Or Something To Avoid Altogether?

38. Is It Possible To Earn Wages And Salaries And Still Create #Value In Assets And Wealth On Your Free Time?

39. Which One Would Allow You To Earn Unlimited Income Even When You're Sick Or Disabled, Assets Or Paychecks?

40. Would You Pass The Knowledge Acquired From This Book On To Your Family And The Next Generation?

Remember   Creating Value And Solving Problems Are, Arguably, The Most Certain Pathways To Truly Achieve Yours Dreams

THE BLUEPRINT

FINANCIAL FREEDOM

Be Industrious

FOLLOW YOUR DREAM

The Workbook

Answers

1. Individual choice.

2. Hint: If it doesn't scare you, it's probably not BIG enough.

3. A property (product or service) which brings you income periodically. Examples: Rental real estate, commercial vehicle or machinery, a business, etc.

4. Brings income periodically.

5. A property which doesn't bring you income periodically. Examples: Your residential home, your private car or truck, etc.

6. Liability takes money away from you regularly.

7. That allows you to build wealth, which provides you income with or without your daily physical involvement.

8. Purpose is primarily about solving a problem which afflicts other people.

9. What common problem are you going to solve?

10. Problems are situations which adversely affect other people or organizations.

11. Problems present opportunities for human progress. Avoidance, rather than solving them, leads to a lack of progress.

12. Problems abound everywhere. Pick the one you're most passionate about.

13. Why not you?

14. Yes? No?

15. It depends on the nature of the problem. Hint: Research the problem.

16. It depends on the nature of the problem. Hint: Research the problem.

17. Yes! If that's what it takes.

18. Researching the problem? Why it exists? Why no one has solved it yet, etc?

19. Yes? No?

20. Yes? No? Hints: Teamwork is essential for success. Two heads are better than one. Spread risks, etc.

21. Mostly

22. Crowd-funding is a great resource, depending on the type of project.

23. Maintaining good credit is absolutely essential.

24. Yes? No? Hints: No scamming, environmental destruction, etc. Remember that you are trying to solve problems, not create more.

25. Makes you a productive citizen, provides sense of fulfilment, builds wealth for self and family leading to financial security and freedom, even for future generations.

26. Yes? No? Hint: Often yes.

27. Yes? No? Hint: Quality sells everywhere. Commit!

28. Yes? No? Hint: Be patient, but persistent. Projects usually take longer than initial estimates.

29. Having others (teammates, family) hold you accountable, tracking #DailyProgress, etc.

30. Personal Initiative, Persistence, hardworking, sense of commitment, positive mental attitude, etc.

31. Yes? No? Hint: Absolutely essential for success.

32. Yes!

33. Yes? No? Hint: Helping others brings joy and deeper meaning to your own life.

34. Formal education provides the training to successfully perform tasks for which you were educated, better than could someone without that particular training.

35. With Financial Education, you're learning how wealthy people became wealthy, and how you could also follow the principles to become wealthy as well.

36. Failure is a natural by-product of trying something new, a vital part of the learning process. It broadens your knowledge and experience on what works and what doesn't.

37. Intelligent (calculated) risk-taking is absolutely necessary for success.

38. Working at a job and creating assets on your free time back at home is totally possible and absolutely necessary for building wealth. The job could provide essential experience and income while working on your dreams or project.

39. Asset is THE KEY.

40. Knowledge is power. Share it.

Remember Creating value and solving problems are, arguably, the most certain pathways to truly achieve your dreams.

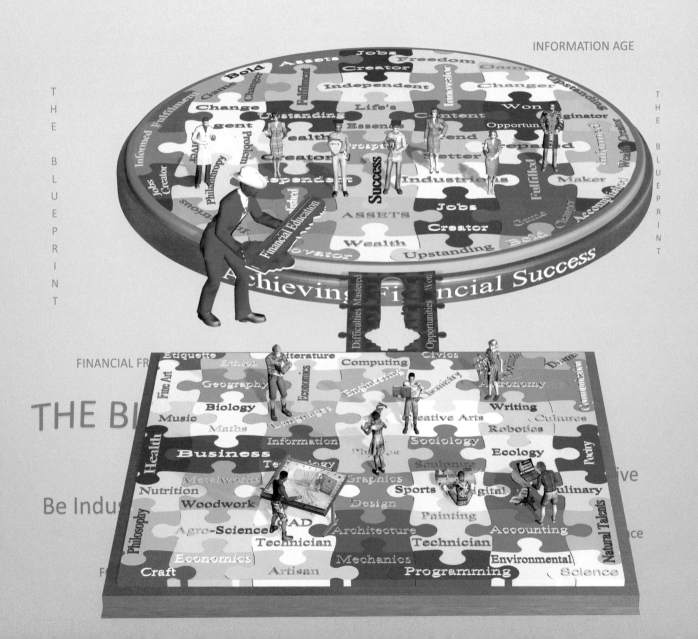

Dream no small dreams for they have no power to move the hearts of men.

...Johann Wolfgang von Goethe

NURTURING THE AMERICAN DREAM

Have you ever wondered why so many people struggle to make ends meet, while a few [rich] people earn lots of money? Do you ever wonder what the #AmericanDream is, and what you can do to achieve it?

Education is THE KEY to success (i.e. mastery) in any field of your choice. Financial Education is THE KEY to your Financial Success. In order to build wealth for yourself and your family, and avoid Financial Struggle when you're older, you need Financial Education in addition to your regular school curriculums.

This book series is absolutely a must-read, insightful blueprint. It will provide you with the nitty-gritty information on the economy, how it works, and what you must do to reach your highest potential and achieve the #AmericanDream through problem-solving and creating value. Prepare to be inspired to Think BIG, Dream even BIGGER, and #BELIEVE that if you can dream it, you [yes, #YOU] can make it happen.

AUTHOR'S BIOGRAPHY

Frank Adjei-Mensah (Uncle Frank) is the author of The American Dream Declassified, published in July, 2014. He has a Bachelor's degree in Law & Sociology, and is also a nurse. He is married with a young family.

Uncle Frank is also an inspirational public speaker and has delivered many lectures on various socio-economic topics at seminars. When he's not at work or glued to the computer working on book projects, he donates his time helping his local church, very dear to him, not to mention the fun times he enjoys with his family.

NURTURING THE AMERICAN DREAM

Have you ever wondered why so many people struggle to make ends meet, while a few [rich] people earn lots of money? Do you ever wonder what the #AmericanDream is, and what you can do to achieve it?

Education is THE KEY to success (i.e. mastery) in any field of your choice. Financial Education is THE KEY to your Financial Success.

This book series is absolutely a must-read, insightful blueprint. It will provide you with the nitty-gritty information on the economy, how it works, and what you must do to reach your highest potential and achieve the #AmericanDream through problem-solving and creating value. Prepare to be inspired to Think BIG, dream even BIGGER, and #BELIEVE that if you can dream it, you [yes, #YOU] can make it happen.

NURTURING
The
American Dream

Frank PN Adjei-Mensah

authorHOUSE

Notes

NURTURE THE DREAM

ASSETS

Aim High

Turn Ideas into Income

INFORMATION AGE

Innovate

Think BIG

Dream even BIGGER

THE BLUEPRINT

THE BLUEPRINT

ASSETS
ACQUISITION

FINANCIAL FREEDOM

Creativity

THE BLUEPRINT

Imaginative

Be Industrious

Persist with diligence

FOLLOW YOUR DREAMS

Be Bold

NURTURE THE DREAM

ASSETS

Aim High

Turn Ideas into Income

INFORMATION AGE

Innovate

B
L
U
E
P
R
I
N
T

T
H
E

Think BIG

B
L
U
E
P
R
I
N
T

T
H
E

Dream even
BIGGER

ASSETS
ACQUISITION

Creativity

FINANCIAL FREEDOM

THE
BLUEPRINT

Imaginative

Be Industrious

Persist with diligence

FOLLOW YOUR DREAMS

Be Bold

Printed in the United States
by Baker & Taylor Publisher Services